# LETTER TO W.H. AUDEN
## And Other Poems
### 1941-1984

*For*

KEN THOMSON

*Other books by the same author include:*

Kafka (1967)
Swansong (Poems, illustrated by Sir Sidney Nolan: 1968)
The Complete Operas of Verdi (1969)
Ned Kelly (1970)
The Concert Song Companion (1974)
Wagner and his World (1977)
Verdi (1977)
The Complete Operas of Mozart (1978)
W. H. Auden: The Life of a Poet (1979)
The Complete Operas of Puccini (1981)
The Life and Crimes of Agatha Christie (1982)
How to Enjoy Opera (1983)
The Dictionary of Opera (1983)

# Letter to W. H. Auden and other poems 1941-1984

C H A R L E S   O S B O R N E

John Calder · London

Riverrun Press · New York

First published in 1984 by
John Calder (Publishers) Limited
18 Brewer Street London W1R 4AS
and by
Riverrun Press Inc
175 Fifth Avenue New York NY 10010

*British Library Cataloguing in Publication Data*
Osborne, Charles, *1927-*

> SUBSIDISED BY THE
> **Arts Council**
> OF GREAT BRITAIN

Letter to W. H. Auden And Other Poems 1941–84.
I. Title
821'.914      PR6065.S15


*Library of Congress Cataloguing in Publication Data*
Osborne, Charles, 1927-

Letter to W. H. Auden And Other Poems 1941-1984.
I. Title.
PR6065. S15A17  1984        821'.914        84–6926


ISBN O-7145-4036-6

Printed and bound in Great Britain by Hillman Printers (Frome) Ltd, Somerset

# CONTENTS

ACKNOWLEDGEMENTS

Some of the poems in this volume first appeared in one or other of the following magazines or anthologies: *The Times Literary Supplement, Sunday Times, The Guardian, New Statesman, London Magazine, Quarto, Outposts, The Bulletin* (Sydney), *Ern Malley's Journal* (Melbourne); *The Oxford Book of Australian Verse* (1956), *Australian Poetry 1951-52, The Queensland Centenary Anthology* (1959), *Australian Poetry 1964, Australian Writing Today* (Penguin: 1968).

# LETTER TO W. H. AUDEN

Dear Wystan, I begin with a confession:
I don't know how to put this, but I must.
You're not likely to pardon this transgression,
Perhaps you'll say I have betrayed your trust,
Although, in my view, that would be unjust.
Ah, well, I'd better get it off my chest,
And hope you'll think I've acted for the best.


The fact is that I'm writing a huge book
About you — it's a kind 'Life and Works' —
In which I aim to take a searching look
At all your poems, books and plays, your quirks
Of personality. I'll get my perks
From reading all your thirties poems again,
To do which I've, for years now, had a yen.


Do you remember, twenty years ago,
When we'd just met, I talked to you of how
I first approached your work, and got to know
F.6, 'Look, Stranger, at this island now',
*The Orators*, the Iceland book? The row
With my old English master at my school
In Brisbane, who denounced you as a fool?

During the war, it was. I was fourteen
There was a blond lad in the class above
Who loaned me books by you, in hopes to wean
Me from the childish verse I used to love.
I must admit he gave me quite a shove
Away from all those Georgians and their charms
Into the modern movement, and your arms.


I use 'your arms' as metaphor, of course.
In fact, the arms he steered me to were his.
As I recall, it didn't take much force:
Boys will be boys. *You* know that, Uncle Wiz.
And other poets, too, he taught me, *viz*
Spender, Day Lewis, Eliot and Yeats.
Those Georgian Brookes and Squires became my hates.


The voice I most responded to was yours,
Although I liked both Spender and Day Lewis.
Eliot I thought too cerebral. 'He bores
The balls right off me', I said to the Jewess
My mother hoped I'd one day marry, who is
A lady who has no place in this letter.
(I hear you mutter: 'Now he's gone all heter!')


Within a year I'd started writing verse,
And soon began to publish in Australia.
My mother thought it such a dreadful curse
And told me, 'As a poet, you're a failure.'
A friend sneered, 'If yer think I'm gunna hail yer
As a new Henry Lawson, jes' fergit it.'
Dad said, 'It'll depress you if you let it.'

None of my friends supported me at all.
They all considered publishing quite boring
And claimed to be astounded at my gall:
They said that after false gods I was whoring.
To them, poems just *were*. This produced soaring
Rage in me, for I liked to be applauded:
Something which they dismissed as being sordid.


Nevertheless I preserved, and soon
Began to be acknowledged as a poet,
Not of the kind that rhymes, like moon with June,
But one whose style was somewhat more inchoate:
'Audenish', someone said. Wouldn't you know it!
I wasn't thrilled to be compared with Auden;
That comment made me feel like Lizzie Borden.


Don't think that what I'm saying is I blame you
For all that verse I scribbled in my teens.
Rather, I'm grateful to you for the fame you
Brought me in Australasia. All that means,
Really, is that I'm one of those has-beens
Who, fêted as a poet when quite young,
Alas, no longer hears his praises sung.


I mention these credentials just because
You once said I'd an honest lyric gift.
That's something I've remembered: it still gnaws
At me as I produce this doggerel, miffed
That *you* praised *my* work. That gives me a lift,
And helps me find the courage now to say
Why I should write a book on Wystan A.

I think, as I read over that last verse,
That 'miffed's a word I may have got all wrong.
I'll look it up — I've known you get quite terse
When friends make verbal slips — it won't take long.
Ah yes, my OED suggests a song
And dance of rage, or getting very huffy,
Or acting in a manner rather stuffy,


Which wasn't what I meant to say at all.
'Chuffed' was the word I wanted, meaning 'pleased',
Though p'raps both 'chuffed' and 'miffed' will quite appal
You with their slangy chirpiness. I've teased
Sufficient mileage out of this, and seized
The opportunity to blow my trumpet.
Oh God, I can't use 'crumpet': let's just dump it,


And talk of something else! This book I'm writing
Is one for which my publishers have pleaded.
At first, although the prospect was exciting,
And your biography is clearly needed,
I shied away from doing it, and ceded
All rights to someone closer to your age,
Sweet saintly Stephen, sterling silver sage.


But it was not to be; he wasn't willing
To undertake the task, so once again
Those wretched publishers all started milling
Around me, pushing dollars at me, Yen,
Lire and Deutschmarks (They're such generous men).
*Post mortem* opposition on your part,
Which seemed to me quite likely, for a start,

They suavely brushed aside, and thrust upon me
A huge advance of several thousand quid
(At least, to me it's huge: they tried to con me
Into accepting less. I almost did.)
And then some other outfit topped their bid.
To one who's usually offered by Gollancz
A mere two thousand, doubled by the Yanks

To four, this represented quite a treasure;
To spurn it, I would have to be a fool.
And, in return, I give myself the pleasure
Of writing about you. That's rather cool,
It seems to me. I've made myself a rule
To write at least five hundred words each morning.
Does that seem quite a lot? I find I'm spawning

Much more than that. It flows out from my pen,
At least the first part does, about your youth.
I'll soon have reached the point where you and Ben
Are introduced by Basil Wright. The truth
Is that I almost fear it's quite uncouth
Of me to take such pleasure in this task.
I sit down at my desk and simply bask

In radiant contentment at the thought
Of what the book will be like. It's the pride
That goes before a fall. Will I be taught
A lesson by reviewers? Will my hide
Be tanned by critics petulant and snide?
No doubt it will: they harbour such resentment.
And what price then my radiant contentment?

Most of the critics, really, pose no problem,
Excepting one, well known as a *Schlemiel.*
I know the usual method is to nobble 'em
And buy 'em off. It costs only a meal
Or two to set up quite a cosy deal
By which one is assured a good review
By all of Grub Street, stretched out in a queue.


Amongst them there's a funny little man
Called Waugh. For years he's been obsessed with me;
Son of the novelist, and an also-ran
Who writes of books, although he's all at sea
When faced with poetry: he'd rather be
Scribbling his own schoolboyish little jokes
Or propping up a bar with all those soaks


On *The Spectator* or, worse, *Private Eye.*
The first has more employees than subscribers,
The latter I don't read — I'd rather die —
I'm told its staff of hacks are all imbibers
Of grape and grain, not strong on moral fibres.
But, to go back to this poor Waugh-like twit
Who, when he hears my name, throws a small fit:


His archilochian satire does no harm,
Abderitan though it is thought by all.
The old Crommyonian sow appears quite calm
Compared with Richard Ingrams whose sheer gall
Keeps *Private Eye* from going to the wall.
A pox upon 'em both: *arcades ambo,*
The silliest duo since Verlaine and Rimbaud.

Some of those words I've put in to amuse you,
In hopes that they're sufficiently arcane;
Others, I know, will make you blow a fuse: you
Once told me there were phrases you'd not deign
To utter; that to hear them gave you pain.
My rhyming, though, we once agreed, dear Wystan,
Is neater than Isolde used on Tristan.


Verlaine, some lines back, calls to mind the time
I asked you if you knew his favourite song.
You thought a while — it really was a crime
To make you ponder quite so hard and long —
And then came up with Fauré's 'Lydia'. Wrong.
'I'm always chasing Rimbaud' was the answer,
At which, in comic rage, like a mad dancer,


You whirled about the room, shaking with laughter,
And then began to plan a party game
Inventing likely favourites; and, soon after,
We tried them all out on your guests who came
To dinner. One extremely grand old dame —
Her name I can't recall — she came from Wien —
Told you she thought the Rimbaud joke obscene.


I've got side-tracked. My Wystan-Tristan rhyme
(Lifted, of course, from your book of graffiti)
Was meant to introduce that pantomime
Dame, Richard Wagner, whom we both thought meaty
But overbearing. 'Oh, come off it, sweetie',
I hear you rasp, 'take it from your old mother,
*Parsifal's* boring. Here, let's have another

Vodka martini.' And, one day, we played,
Chester and you and I, the game of choosing
Funeral music for ourselves. I made
Mahler my choice, but I was quickly losing
All self-restraint due to the heavy boozing
We were indulging in. Chester, I think,
Announced, as he poured out another drink,


That he'd be buried to the sound of Verdi.
I seem to hear him ask for 'Va, pensiero'.
Knowing your views on that, I'd not have dared. He
Must have been kidding. 'I shall die a hero',
You then announced, striking a pose like Nero,
'And a real hero's music there must be.
Nothing but Siegfried's Funeral March for me.'


We were all joking, I've no doubt of that,
But one day, ten years later, in your house,
Close by the Wiener Wald, your friends all sat,
Mourning your death, while, outside, not a mouse
Stirred in the woods or garden. Sounds of Strauss
Floated across the fields, then Chester rose
And murmured softly, 'Before Wystan goes


From this house for the last time, there's one thing
I must do. Now I want you all to rise.'
We stood, and let dead Siegfried's music ring
Throughout the house: the tears flowed from our eyes.
Was I the only one to recognize
We wept because old Wagner told us to?
We loved, so had no need to weep for, you.

Although it's shorter than your screed to Byron
This letter is already far too long.
In writing it, I've made you seem a siren
Luring me from my work. I'll end this song,
And hope you don't think mail from live friends wrong.
As to its length, I tell myself you'll need it.
You've all eternity in which to read it.

This poem was written in 1978, while I was at work on
my biography of W. H Auden.

# THE FRENZIED BOAT

**A Version of
Arthur Rimbaud's**
*Le Bateau Ivre*

As I sailed on, down the impassive rivers,
I felt the boatmen hauling me no more:
Redskins, screaming, had pounced on them for targets,
Tying them naked to coloured stakes.


Carrier of Flemish corn or English cotton,
I now forgot completely all my crew;
And when the uproar finished with my haulers
The rivers let me drift on where I wished.


That other winter, duller than children's brains
I coursed, through the ferocious swelling
Of the tides! And the unmoored Peninsulas
Had never suffered such triumphant chaos.


The tempest blessed my maritime awakenings:
Lighter than a cork I danced along the waves
Which some call ceaseless carriers of prey,
For ten nights, with no foolish  winking lantern.


Sweeter than firm apple's pulp to children,
The green sea seeped into my hull of pine,
Washing me clean from rough wine-stains
And vomitings, dispersing my helm and grappling.

And ever since then, bogged down in the poem
Of the lactescent sea, infused by stars,
I have consumed its azure depths where, gaunt
And pallid flotsam, a pensive drowned man sinks;


Where, staining suddenly those slow blue rhythms,
Delirious beneath the gleaming of the day,
Stronger than alcohol, more spacious than your song
The red and bitter wounds of love ferment.


I know skies cracked by lightning, water spouts,
The undertows and currents; I know evening,
And dawn exalted like a flock of doves.
I've sometimes seen what man believes he saw.


I saw the low sun stained with mystic horrors
Light up coagulated violet shapes,
Like actors in a very ancient drama,
While distant rolling waves quivered, like blinds.


I dreamed, all green night long, of dazzling snow,
Of languid kisses offered to the sea,
The circulation of unheard-of saps,
And warnings, yellow, blue, by phosphorous singers.


For months on end I followed close the waves
Which stormed the reefs like maddened, stamping herds,
Not dreaming that the Mary's luminous feet
Could overcome the muffled ocean's wheeze.

You know, I've knocked against incredible Floridas,
Their flowers reflected in the eyes of panthers wearing skins
Of men; and against rainbows hanging like bridles
For glaucous herds, below the sea's horizon.


I've seen marshes fermenting, enormous fish-nets
Where, in the reeds, an entire Leviathan rots;
The seas collapsing in the midst of calm,
And the distances, cascading the ravines.


Glaciers, silver suns, pearly waves and glowing skies,
Hideous groundings in dark chasms' depths
Where giant serpents, devoured by bugs,
Fall from trees twisted with black perfumes.


I would have liked to show children those dolphins
Of the blue waves, those golden, singing fish;
Flowers of foam have blessed my putting out to sea,
And ineffable winds have sometimes lent me wings.


Sometimes, that martyr weary of poles and zones,
The sea, whose sobbing lightened my rolling,
Would lift up to me its shadowy yellow-suckered flowers,
And I would be still, like a woman on her knees.


Almost an island, I tossed on my beaches the quarrels
And the dung of screeching, pale-eyed birds,
And I sailed on when, through my frail rigging,
Drowned men sank backwards down to sleep.

Now I, ship lost in the hair of inlets,
Flung by the hurricane into the birdless ether,
I, whose carcass drunk with water neither Monitors
Nor Hanseatic schooners would have salvaged;


I who, free, reeking, rising from purple mists,
Have pierced the sky which reddens like a wall
Carrying moss from the sun and mucus from the blue,
Exquisite preserve of first-rate poets;


Who raced on, stained by electric moons,
Mad hulk escorted by black sea horses,
While July's heat with its cudgelling blows destroyed
The glowing craters of the lapis lazuli sky;


I, who trembled, hearing across fifty leagues
Behemoths and Maelstroms whining in heat,
Eternal spinner of the immobile blue,
I miss the ancient parapets of Europe.


I saw sidereal archipelagoes and islands
Whose frenzied skies lie open to the sailor:
Are these your endless nights of sleeps and exile,
O million golden birds, O future vigour?


It's true I've wept too much. The dawns are heart-rending,
Each moon atrocious, and each sun so bitter.
I'm bloated with the intoxicating fumes of aerial love.
O, let my keel splinter, let me flounder in the sea.

If I desire any water of Europe, it is the cold
Black puddle where, in the scented dusk,
A child, heavy with sadness, crouches to launch
A boat frail as a butterfly in May.


Steeped in your languors, o waves, I can no longer
Pick up the cotton merchant's wake,
Nor thwart the pride of flags and pennants,
Nor swim beneath the frightful eyes of hulks.

This version of Rimbaud was made for Sir Sidney Nolan. It was in 1947 that he and I
first talked of the *Bateau Ivre,* on a Pacific beach.

# OTHER POEMS

# FOR NOLAN AT FIFTY

You painted landscape, people, skies
and distant prospects, tenderly:
dark men walked naked from the sea
for you, who painted memory.


Sun-dancing beaches, outback pubs,
sad oval faces, all conspired
to tempt you into knowing them.
Square-headed outlaws used to ride


Through bush. But that was long ago,
and in another country too,
where fifty suns blaze in the sky,
and birds fly upside down for you.

## ARCTIC ANIMALS IN WINTER DRESS (or NATURE PLAYS FAIR)

Many northern animals,
inhabiting regions
which are free from snow
during part of the year,
undergo a seasonal
change of colour,
being dark in summer,
and almost or entirely
white in winter.


This change of colour
not only helps to conceal
herbivorous species
from their enemies,
but also enables
carnivorous animals
to approach their prey
unperceived.

A *poéme trouvé* from the museum at Exeter.

## THE AGED ACTOR SPEAKS

I'm having a sale of old memories.
Perhaps you'd like to buy one or two?


This one, for instance.
I know it's somewhat faded, and it has a few patches in it.
Yes, I did those myself, though I hadn't really meant to.
I'm not terribly fond of it now,
but it's certainly more serviceable than when it was new.


Here is another. Now this I really don't want to part with,
but, for reasons of health, I'm told I must.
Yes, it's in perfect condition. I've always kept it that way,
yet I've used it so often.
I can't think what I shall do without it, but I'm told I must.


And of course this one, which I suppose I ought to
share with you. It really belonged to us both. Oh, you don't
think so? But surely you remember?

I see, you just don't want your part of it.
Perhaps, then, I can let it go to someone else,
though that doesn't seem right to me.


What will you give me for the lot? Yes, all of them.
It's just that I can't bear to pick them out and dwell on them.
I offer them all. What do you think they're worth?


No more than that? But surely —
Yes, but don't you understand? They are my own, they are unique,
they're very precious.


I don't feel I could bear to part with them so cheaply.
And so, although I'm told that soon I shall have nowhere
to keep them properly, I think that, perhaps, for the time being
I shall hold on to them.
Yes, hold on to them, that's what I'll do.
You see, there's nothing else,
they're really all I have.

## A POP SONG FOR SADIE

If you were a flower, you'd be a crimson rosebud,
if you were a bird, a cooing turtle-dove,
if you were a poem, you'd be by Keats or Shelley,
a colour, silver as the moon above,

If you were to eat, you'd be a bowl of cherries,
a month, you'd be the sunny days of June,
if you were a singer, you'd be Judy Garland,
if you were a song, then Gershwin wrote your tune.

If you were a planet, you'd be none but Venus,
If you were a waltz, you'd be the best of Strauss,
If you were a city, you'd be San Francisco,
a cartoon character, you're Minnie Mouse.

If you were a boy, I'd change my sex for you, dear,
if you were a ghost, I'd die, to be one, too,
if you were a dream, I'd hope never to waken
so thank Christ, sweetheart, you are only you.

## STRINGYBARK
(a fragment)

Four of them rode away, that day,
Under a summer sky,
Carrying rifles on their backs.
Kelly, they said, must die.

Ned and his three mates kept alert,
Eager to join the fight.
Dan, Joey Byrne, and young Steve Hart
Knew all the police by sight.

Evening it was, at Stringybark,
Light faded from the sky.
Lonigan, drowsing by the fire,
Yawned, while the gang passed by.

I passed this off as the beginning of a nineteenth-century ballad about the Kelly gang, and included it in the appendix of a book I wrote about Ned Kelly, which was published in 1970. Its acrostic message went unnoticed at the time.

## PRIVATE JOURNEY

We had gone some miles that day
far into the bush.
Our journey had become a dream,
and I seem to remember
I was trying to write a poem
as we walked.
Problems of technique
had engaged my thinking,
but as we entered the dream
I turned and stared at my companion
to see if he looked
changed or unfamiliar
when he was dreaming.

He was speaking to me
but I could not hear his words,
and I connected this disability
with the great distance we had travelled.
'There is only one journey I ever make',
I reflected,
'and it is deep into myself.
I have travelled so far today
that now I am alone.'

35

I was distressed at this:
I always had a fear
of loneliness, and now that the
smiling image of my friend
was fading with his voice
I began to feel desolate,
and to be sorry to have landed myself
in so familiar and desperate a plight.
I remember being consoled, however,
that, although I was alone with my dream,
I was deep within the bush,
and not in my narrow bed.


(In this eternal jungle
we have rehearsed our love,
I have confessed this
pensive whoredom of the heart
from which I suffer now,
and to which you turn,
expecting gentleness;
can you not see me then,
my eyes over your shoulder and away,
speaking so elsewhere these only words:


Sometimes the only answer is a tear,
the silence heavy with regret.
Should the question have been asked?
And in that time, shall we affirm
that once we loved and were
afraid to love,
and now,
both lonely and aware

must live
within our dream?)


I wondered if
speaking these words aloud,
as I stumbled on, I somehow knew
the more I spoke,
the more alone I should be.
I resolved to make no sound,
hoping that soon my friend
would appear at my side again.
I knew that without him
I should stay lost
in the outback of my dream.


And from that moment
I walked
in silence.

# LITERARY SQUABBLES

i

Ah God! the petty fools of rhyme
That shriek and sweat in pigmy wars
Before the stony face of Time,
And look'd at by the silent stars:

Who hate each other for a song,
And do their little best to bite
And pinch their brethren in the throng,
And scratch the very dead for spite:

And strain to make an inch of room
For their sweet selves, and cannot hear
The sullen Lethe rolling doom
On them and theirs and all things here:

When one small touch of Charity
Could lift them nearer God-like state
Than if the crowded Orb should cry
Like those who cried Diana great:

And I too, talk, and lose the touch
I talk of. Surely, after all,
The noblest answer unto such
Is perfect stillness when they brawl.


ii


Yes, perfect stillness has its use,
No doubt, although I cannot stand
Mutely to suffer fools' abuse.
No cheek I'll turn, rather my hand


Against the cheeky ones who scream
Petulantly unless I share
Their high opinion of a team
Of friends whom they would publish. Dare


I say these self-appointed hacks-
Turned-publishers are almost worse
Than those they carry on their backs,
Purveyors of atrocious verse?


More loathesome still, I think, are those
Who write me in offensive terms,
And then complain in pompous prose
Whenever I attack the worms

In equally abrasive style.
'How dare a public servant write
Such words to me?' Out spills the bile;
The squabble's now a full-blown fight.

This poem is a work of collaboration. Alfred, Lord Tennyson wrote the first part, and I, more than a hundred years later, in my persona of Literature Director of the Arts Council of Great Britain, the second.

## GUY

So I sit here and watch them watching me.
They think I'm sullen. I suppose I am,
Only because I don't get angry any more.
When I screamed at them, they laughed

And were frightened. And threw things.
Now I sit and look and do not see them.
I see only what is in my memory, green
And yellow, cool heat, lethargy and the flesh.

Sometimes I am stirred into the present
As one, darker than the others, wanders past.
My eyes follow him, and I hear them say
'See how his eyes are following.'

Remembering life, I occasionally play
With myself. 'He's well made, isn't he?'
When I made a mess they laughed
And were disgusted. 'Filthy beast.'

So I sit, watching, remembering, not
Seeing. Unamused, so unamusing. Neither
moving nor moved when they murmur
'He's getting old, that's when they're dangerous.'

This was written on Guy Fawkes' Day, 1963, after I had visited Guy, the gorilla, at
London Zoo.

# THE SMILE

The Poet's vacant
and engaging smile
is even falser now
than once it was.

Ingredients: love,
mirror, hate and cold.
(Amused self-pity
is an added spice.)

He's bored and fretful,
lazy, gentle, proud,
And anxious. Frightened.
Scared to death of life.

The Nolan drawing on the front cover was made to illustrate this poem. Also see pp. 314-5 of *W. H. Auden: The Life of a Poet* by Charles Osborne (New York, 1979; London 1980).

## SWANSONG
## (a cantata)

*aria:*
Old swan you are sad
swimming slow to the shore,
black swan what hurts you
and where is your love?

*recitative:*
I have no love
and yet it is my love that hurts.

*aria:*
Black swan you are ill
sitting there on the shore,
old swan sick and lonely
swim back to your love.

*recitative:*
My love has gone to another,
leave me to weep.

*aria:*

My swan there is blood
flowing down from your breast,
swan lover your heart bleeds,
I fear you will die.

*recitative:*

My heart is breaking
and my love flows away.
Without my love
yes I shall die.

I had read a news item in *The Times*, sometime in 1950, about a male swan pining for
his mate who had left him. The swan refused to eat, and died.

45

## SONG OF NOTHING

Why then there's
nothing.
A family of swans
on the river Dart,
a field being ploughed,
ever and silent the hills,
and in my heart
no, there's nothing.


Why then there's
nothing.
The wild wild flowers
shivering in the world,
outside my ears
the flapping of wings,
and within
no, there's nothing.


Why then there's
nothing.
The laughter of a bird
high from the world,
someone to love
for the moment in time,
and in my heart there's —
no, there's nothing.

## DREAM LANDSCAPE

There is a landscape in my dream
for only you to walk through,
o my remorseless and most injured love.
There is a sea, all green and waves,
porpoises, and ships for chariots,
and such a distance that your eye
will laugh at. You will clap your hands.
All clouds to heaven will go singing,
and you alone,
calm and smiling in that fragile hour,
will walk out of a cold, clear morning,
into the landscape and my dream.

# THREE FOOLS WAVING

Where I am here
your voice,
a smile identified
and three fools
waving.

Soft now
coastline of my dream,
your tears
inflexible and graceful
words in my heart.

Stillness
where I was,
our gentle planet
and the night time
ever moving.

## MAP OF A COUNTRY

I saw my country
like a strange sad star
dreaming within a dream,
lost in an ocean,
found on the map
of love.


Here in my country
mountains are,
tears and rivers,
trees and laughter,
forest, passion
and the desert.


Away from my country
I am nowhere,
I cannot be lost
but I must lie
near sand and ocean,
between tears and silence.

## TO TRUTH

MAP OF A COUNTRY

So fly by night,
my phrase will not pursue you
through darkness and the
evil that men do.
Your flirting breath may dance
on time and passion,
or hide from sorrow
in a word or two.

But don't be sad
for gentleness surrounds you,
and though I move without
your gay deceit,
I know that you with time
and love will find me,
and bless, promiscuous truth,
the day we meet.

# FOLK SONGS FROM AN UNKNOWN COUNTRY

i

Do you belong to the twilight
or will you come back to me?
Are you forever my sweetheart
whose shadow in dreams I see?


You whom I kiss so gently,
do you belong to me
or are you a part of the night time,
are you the moon's memory?


Farewell, my passionate shadow,
your love like a star and a tree
will smile on and ease all my sadness,
and you will remember me.

ii

Up jumped down sprang
all around the world sang,
bird flies swiftly
all around the world.


Gun so sharp rang
all around the world sang,
bird falls slowly
all around the world.


Sadly clouds hang,
all around the world sang,
bird lies dying
all around the world.

# OTHER TRANSLATIONS

OTHER TRANSLATIONS

## WANDERER'S NIGHT SONG (Goethe)

Over all the mountains
is peace,
in all the tree-tops
you feel
hardly a breath.
The little birds are silent in the woods.
Wait awhile:
soon
you too will rest.

## GANYMEDE (Goethe)

How you glow upon me
in the morning's radiance,
my beloved Spring.
Love with its thousand delights
is thrust into my heart
by your eternal warmth,
your beauty sacred
and enduring.

O that I might clasp you
in my arms.


See, on your breast
I lie and swoon,
your foliage, flowers,
pressed closely to my heart.
You cool the burning
thirst of my breast,
sweet morning breeze.
Now the nightingale calls
lovingly to me from the valley's mist.


I come, I come,
but, tell me, where?
Up there, Upwards I strive.
The clouds are floating
down to me, the clouds
bow down to my yearning love.
To me! To me!
Held in your lap,
carried above,
clasping and clasped,
upwards to your bosom,
all-loving Father.

## QUITE FAIR (Eluard)

It is the burning law of men
from grapes they make wine
From coal they make fire
From kisses they make men

It is the hard law of men
To keep themselves secure
From wars and misery
And the dangers of death

It is the sweet law of men
Changing water into light
Dream to reality
And enemies into friends

This law both old and new
Which moves towards perfection
From deep in the heart of the child
To the heights of reason.

## THE UNFAITHFUL WIFE (Lorca)

And thinking she was a virgin
I took her down to the river —
but she was a married woman.

It was St. James' night,
it could almost have been arranged.
The lamps were out
but the crickets were glowing.
In a dark spot
I touched her dormant breasts
and they blossomed to my hand
as sprigs of hyacinth.
The starch in her underskirt
sounded to my ears
like a piece of silk
torn by ten knives.

Now that no light shone,
the trees loomed larger,
and far from the river
dogs barked the whole horizon of our ears.

We passed the bushes,
the reeds and the fern,
her long dark hair
hollowed in the earth.
I took off my tie.
She took off her dress.
I removed my revolver-belt.
She her four bodices.
Her skin was finer
than the snail,
shining on the moon
brighter than any jewel.
Her thighs sped from me
like startled fish,
half fiery
and half cold.
That night I travelled the most comfortable road
astride my sweet mare
without saddle or stirrup.


As a man, I shan't repeat
the things she said to me.
The light of understanding
has shown me discretion.
Covered with sand and her kisses
I carried her from the river.
The lilies crossed swords
emboldened by the wind.

I behaved as I should have,
like a proper gypsy.
I gave her a sewing box,
a large one, all satin,
and I tried not to love her
since she was married,
though she told me she was a virgin
when I took her down to the river.

**CHILD'S SONG** (Borchert)


Mama, where does God live?
My darling, in the moat.


What's he do there?


He teaches little fish to swim
So they don't have to float.


Mama, where does God live?
He lives out in the stall.


What's he do there?


He taught our little calf to walk,
so that he doesn't fall.

## FAREWELL (Borchert)

Our last kiss
by the quay
was over.

You sailed
downstream
to the sea.

I watched the
light now red
now green
slowly
withdraw.

CHILD'S SONG (Borchert)

Mama, where does God live?
My darling, in the moat.

Where's he do there?

He watches little fish no swim.
So they don't have to float.

Mama, where does God live?
He lives out in the stall.

Where's he do there?

He taught our little calf to walk,
so that he doesn't fall.

# I'M THE FIFTH MAN (Jandl)

door opens
one man out
one man in
I'm the fourth man

door opens
one man out
one man in
I'm the third man

door opens
one man out
one man in
I'm the second man

door opens
one man out
one man in
I'm next

door opens
one man out
myself in
'morning, doctor

## ANTIPODES (Jandl)

        a leaf
and under this
        a leaf
and under this
        a leaf
and under this
        a leaf
and under this
        a table
and under this
        a floor
and under this
        a room
and under this
        a cellar
and under this
        a globe
and under this
        a cellar
and under this
        a room

and under this

        a floor

and under this

        a table

and under this

        a leaf

and under this

        a leaf

and under this

        a leaf

and under this

        a leaf

**SPREE IN SPRING** (Jandl)

spree in spring
in spring sum
sum in summer
ought in autumn
in autumn wint
wint in winter
in winter spree

# JUVENILIA

# SWEENEY AND THE NIGHTINGALE

Clear against the moon,
the nightingale sat
on the branch of a dream.
Rapturously alone,
she began to sing
into the night of lovers.


Sweeney,
alone with his love
sauntered past,
stopped to look
into the sky,
and saw the bird,
its song pierced with stars.


Blond and erect
Sweeney,
sad and melodious
the bird.
Her song became love,
her heart beat,
something trembled,
and she looked down

at Sweeney, blond
erect and still.
O nightingale,
whispered Sweeney,
tell me —


If I were not love,
you would be my love,
sang the nightingale.
In the forest of my dreams
you, Sweeney, have been
ever present,
sweet arrow piercing
like a star,
sweet torture to love,
my heart flies down to you.


The bird's song now
more rapturous, now
achieving death-in-love,
sharper against the moon
her gleaming clarity.


O nightingale,
whispered Sweeney,
tell me —
do you eat snakes?

## ON COCTEAU'S DRAWING OF LIFAR ASLEEP

Had you just left him,
sleeping through your dream,
his brow in love with smoothness
and the air,
his hollowed face
poised on the pillow,
his eyes withdrawn
and cheeks articulate,
his mouth still asking you
the only question?


Hands clasped and
clasping his pillow,
he dreams for you
and sleeps with you
while you are smiling
from the distance of your art
(you and he, here
there and now).
Distance is love,
the artist is asleep
and dancing such a dream
that you will smile
again
from your enchanted distance,
and say the rest
is silence.

## IN QUIET DESPERATION

In quiet desperation
fancy free,
we move and
live and have
our being, and
reserve our right to love.

Did we move
backwards
like the knowing crab,
towards love and
atom, shall we forget
to be
or not to be,
are we stretched taut?

Then let us not be quiet
in the sun
nor conceive by the moon,
let us postpone delirium
till the dead of night.

## SONG

Go walkabout my darling
and I am by your side,
my heart is beating with you,
our love is yet untried —


then speak to me my darling
and let our dream begin,
my memory passes over
the moment of our sin —


this time and you will leave me,
my springtime love has died,
go walkabout my darling
with love still by your side.

## EYES

See here in my eyes,
old man, your memory,
but do not see that I
who carry your memory
am also a mirror, cold
and alive.


See what you want, know
where you have been,
and feel no love for me
for I am cold
and wish I were a magic mirror
but know that
magic is cold
my eyes cold
old man cold and looking to
my eyes for what you left there
many times
many years, and
a few kisses, perhaps,
and a gesture of indifferent love.


See here in my face,
old man, only
your urgency as you gaze
upon my lips
which are so sadly alive.

## GEMINIANI AT BRIGHTON

A frightened violin
cries,
and a time is thought of
where music
moving in stillness
will be lonely and alone.


Shall we now
weep
for the fearful sound,
and for ourselves
who have most grievously
never moved
in stillness,
nor heard the lovely noise
of fear?

Brighton: a seaside suburb of Melbourne, not the Sussex Brighton.

# TRIVIA

## BRIGID BROPHY INSTRUCTED ON THE PRONUNCIATION OF 'KOALA'

There was a composer called Mahler
whose premieres were awfully gala:
He'd conduct with his hat on,
And quite without bâton,
Concerti played by a koala.

## THE CASE OF BURT AND ELSA vs THE QUEEN
### (AS REPORTED IN *THE PUSSY-CATS' GAZETTE)*


First the judge spoke: 'O wicked Burt
and Elsa to have done this deed.
Criminal pussies! Pay atten–
–tion to my words. How do you plead?'


Unconcerned, suave, quite at their ease,
licking their paws, the prisoners sat.
'Monsters and rogues', the judge resumed,
'you have disgraced the name of cat.'


Up jumped Patch Cooper, P. C. C.*
'My Lord', he cried, 'there's some mistake.
These harmless dears have done no wrong.'
'No wrong? Did they not steal a cake


made by Charles Osborne (virtuous youth),
and left upon the kitchen chair?
Did they not creep in, unawares,
and take the cake from off of there?'


* Pussy Cats' Counsel

'You can't say "off of", judge', cried Patch,
'it's incorrect, also not true.
The wretched Osborne testifies
not about cakes. He says these two

innocent babes have killed a bird.
What if they have? No harm in that.
There sits the criminal', he yelled,
pointing at Osborne, 'sleek and fat.

Gluttonous, too. Hear what he did,
and then decide. Osborne, the lout,
first stole the bird from these two babes,
then ate it whole. There is no doubt

of that, my Lord, for we'll produce
a witness who will testify
that Osborne here swallowed the bird.
Von Katian* with his own eye

saw all this happen.' 'Yes, indeed',
called out von Katian, 'and you know
I would not lie. My character,
it's often said, is pure as snow.

Pronounced 'Kat-ee-an'

Not only that, I'm also known
as a musician. Bruno Wal-
-ter himself was heard to say
"Long live les Bonchats Musicales".'


'That doesn't scan', Charles Osborne sneered.
'Scan? What is that? Don't try to change
the subject', screeched von Katian.
'The *Bonchats Musicales* arrange — '


'Silence in Court', boomed out the judge,
'Enough of this. Pussies, arise.
**Elsa and Burt, case is dismissed.**
You're free. Osborne, apologize


to these maligned sweet pussies here.
Stop scowling, man, you have no choice.'
'Oh, all right, I apologize.'
Loud cheers in court. 'Pussies, rejoice,


your case is won. Hurrah, hurrah',
the jury cried, by chance composed
of all the *Bonchats Musicales*,
while in the dock the accused both dozed.

They didn't wake, although poor Charles
had picked them up to take them home.
Snug in his arms they lay, and dreamed
of landscape green in which to roam,


and lie and sleep and stretch and yawn.
At home they woke. 'Hush, not a word',
said Elsa. 'Charles has gone to sleep.
Let's go and get another bird.'

This was written in 1958 for Barbara Cooper, my colleague on the staff of
*The London Magazine*. Barbara had a cat named Patch. Burt and Elsa were my two cats,
who had disgraced themselves by stealing a cake and by killing a bird which they
then presented to me. The *Bonchats Musicales*, a cats chorus about which Barbara and I
had many conversations, was conducted by the celebrated Herbert von Katian.

## PASTICHE IMPROVISED IN THE PRESENCE OF OGDEN NASH

I was delighted to be invited to Poetry International
though it seems to me the choice of poets is hardly very rational,
and, what's more, I don't really
understand from looking at the names on the poster whether or not
                                        I'm going to hear Robert Creeley.

Ogden Nash and Robert Creeley both appeared at the poetry festival, *Poetry International* (1969), at my invitation. When Nash drew my attention to a mistake on our poster, I answered him in the style of one of his own poems. He then made me write it down for him, and threatened to claim it as his own. I said I was sure he would do no such thing, since my improvisation was both poor and, out of context, incomprehensible, to which he replied: 'You have described a typical Ogden Nash poem!'

## ON RECEIVING FROM EDWARD LUCIE–SMITH A COPY OF HIS 'BESTIARY'

The Lucie-Smith's a gentle beast
who still observes the Christmas feast
by sending poems to all his friends.
Thus Edward shall restore amends.

# A BAD POEM FOR CARLISLE

How we came here, and why
Or what you expect from us,
Rightly I cannot say.
**Real people disguised as dolls**
Or waxwork figures,
Rigidly you sit, stare,

Casually enter, leave.
And boredom, slashed across your faces,
Rusts into your skin.
Listening, you wonder at the strange
**Intensity that emanates from our nervous voices, our**
**Sallow, metropolitan faces.**
Literary people, you think, are
Elegant but useless, cannot connect with real life.

Melvyn Bragg, Ian Hamilton, Julia Jones, and I sat on a platform somewhere in
Carlisle, addressing an audience which had ventured forth on a very wet winter night
in 1970 to attend an Arts Council 'Writers on Tour' event. The evening went badly,
and while Ian was reading a group of his poems I wrote on a sheet of paper, vertically,
the words 'HORROR CARLISLE' and then scribbled the above instant poem to
fit the initial letters.

**OMAR AND EDWARD** (with grateful acknowledgements to Frank Kermode)


'A jug of wine, a loaf of bread,
these are life's pleasures', Khayyam said.
'A sheep's thigh is a further joy,
and, after food, a pretty boy'.


His devious translator, though,
looked at the poet's list, and 'No',
he said, 'since I have lived without
a taste of meat, I'll make devout


old Persian Omar spurn it too:
a book of verse will have to do.
Though poems the Persians may not heed,
I know best what Victorians read.


For pretty boys I share his taste
but can't admit it — too debased —
and yet I think I've found a way
to let old Omar have his say.'

He took his pen and tried a verse.
'Not bad', he thought, 'it could be worse:
"A flask of wine beneath the bough,
And poetry, and bread — and thou".'

Frank Kermode, sometime in 1962, had reviewed in the *New Statesman* a book on Edward Fitzgerald; it was on reading his review that I wrote the above verses, hence the apparently irrelevant acknowledgement to Frank.

## LIMERICK *À CLEF*

A young man from old Tuscaloosa
Had quite a career as producer
Until, down in Dallas,
He worked with La Callas
And was sacked when he tried to seduce her.

# LETTER TO THE EDITOR

Sir,
If Senator Fulbright told a lie,
it's certain he won't go to heaven;
but, worst of all, if he should die,
he'll not be mourned by Bernard Levin.
Yours etc,

After the Watergate revelations, Bernard Levin published an article in *The Times* suggesting that Nixon was being unfairly treated, and castigating Senator Fulbright for having mentioned a public opinion poll which one of his assistants later said had not been taken.

## LETTER TO A PUBLISHER

(My letter was sent in reply to the following, received from Peter Jay, whose firm had distributed my volume of poems, *Swansong*.

Dear Charles,

                 Between the bills I found your card
Of 2nd. inst., enquiring of the state
Of credit — now touching on sixty quid —
Which IOU for Swansongs sold to date.
Alas! There's less than nothing in my accounts
But I hope soon my cheques will be less bounce-
y, not to mention my rhymes and metre.
See you on May the 12th. — till then,

                 Yours,
                 Peter)


Dear Peter,

                 Though I do not mind at all
the fact you cannot cough up sixty quid,
I really must protest at the appall-
ing stanza which you sent me, and I bid
you not so to offend the ear again
of your friend Charles, most sensitive of men.

## FOR PETER PORTER

I hope it consoles Peter Porter
(Who fears that he's now out of vogue)
to know that, though older than Patten,
he's younger than Christopher Logue.

## THREE SLIGHT AND/OR INCOMPREHENSIBLE
## POEMS FOR GAVIN EWART

i
*NOT AFTER HEINE*

The road to Limerick is paved with Joyces;
In Dublin Bay twelve poets drown one reader.
The dead man's cry is joined by angel voices:
'Please take me to your alten Bösen Leider.'


ii
*A HAIKU ABOUT A LIMERICK*

I am pleased to note
that the Japanese pronounce
it as 'Rim-a-lick.'


(iii)
*A LIMERICK ABOUT A HAIKU*

The poet sat crouched in the loo,
While outside there stretched a long queue.
When they banged on the doors
He cried, 'Don't be such bores.
I'm attempting to write a haiku.'


These three poems were written at the request of Mrs Gavin Ewart
and included in an album of poems given to the poet on his sixty-fifth birthday in
1981. Limericks and Haikus seem to appeal to Gavin, and the first of the three poems
contains several Ewartian allusions.

## GOOD NEWS IN SEPTEMBER 1981

Gavin Ewart, the best poet in Putney, is alive
And kicking, observed his rivals in S.W.5.

This was sent to Gavin Ewart, prince of trivia , after I read in the *London Review of Books* his poem, 'Bad News in April 1981':
Robert Garioch, the best poet in Scotland, is dead.
The wit stops coming from that remarkable singing head.

# CLERIHEW NOT BY W. H. AUDEN

**Melvyn Bragg**
finds it rather a fag
to have to choose a poet;
his mind goes inchoate.

This was scribbled during an Arts Council meeting at which both Melvyn and I were
finding it difficult to choose a bursar from among several poets.